OBSESSIVE COMPULSIVE DISORDERS

Understanding and supporting children with mild obsessive compulsive disorders (OCD)

Rob Long

David Fulton Publishers Ltd
The Chiswick Centre, 414 Chiswick High Road, London W4 5TF

www.fultonpublishers.co.uk

First published in Great Britain by David Fulton Publishers in association
with the National Association for Special Educational Needs (NASEN)

NASEN is a registered charity no. 1007023.

David Fulton Publishers is a division of Granada Learning Limited, part
of ITV plc.

British Library Cataloguing in Publication Data
A catalogue record for this book is available from the British Library.

ISBN 184312 366 5

Typeset by FiSH Books, London
Printed and bound in Great Britain

Contents

Foreword

This booklet has several aims:

1 To raise the understanding of school staff to the nature of obsessive compulsive disorders (OCD) in children and young people
2 To explore a range of interventions
3 To enable school staff to make informed decisions in supporting children and young people who suffer with OCD.

It is not intended to replace referral to a doctor or other health professional but can be used alongside the active involvement of other professionals working to support a child suffering from OCD.

Children who experience severe and disabling forms of obsessive compulsive disorder are quickly referred to mental health professionals for support. Schools are often faced, however, with children and young people who display milder forms of this condition (known as subclinical OCD). Through increased awareness and understanding of the dynamics of obsessive compulsive disorders it is hoped that supporting such children will be less stressful for school staff and more beneficial for the sufferers.

1 Introduction

All children experience situations that naturally make them feel frightened and upset. Up until the age of two, separation anxiety is one such situation, when children become distressed if separated from their carers. This is a normal emotional reaction and is no indication of future problems (in fact it is more a sign for concern when a child does not show any anxiety at being separated). By the age of two, however, most children are able to cope with being out of sight of their carer for short periods of time.

At different ages there are certain 'behavioural rituals' that, while suggestive of OCD, are actually a part of normal development. These may include cuddling favourite toys or blankets when faced with new situations. This would not be unusual for a three-year-old child. However, when a child of eight or nine still experiences the same need, and is anxious if he or she cannot carry out the same routine as before, then this response may be a problem and the child will need understanding and support. As Kendall (2000) puts it, 'there are different fears for different years' – the behaviour is normal for the three-year-old but less so for the eight-year-old.

Common childhood fears and anxieties

Eight months to two years
Separation anxiety – common rituals exist around bedtimes; for example, some children always need the same soft toys placed in the same order.

Two to four years
Imaginary fears – the dark, animals; mild forms of checking such as making sure windows are securely closed; fear of germs and dirt.

Six years on
Fears of injury, death and natural disasters; counting (for example, always counting to a certain number while they are getting dressed) and lucky numbers.

(Kendall, 2000; Thomsen, 2001)

It is common for children aged two or above to develop their own patterns of ritual. Bedtimes are a good example, with children demanding that the same book or page be read even though more interesting stories are available. We can see this as children's way of coping with anxieties – the rituals serve to comfort and distract them from worries. As they grow they develop new and different ways of coping. As with many behaviours there is a continuum which shows this to be normal in certain contexts and at certain stages of development. It is when the behaviour continues into different contexts and/or different ages that it becomes dysfunctional and prevents the child from adapting successfully.

Anxiety and fear are natural, unlearned reactions that warn us that something is not right. They signal a need for action to avoid some threat. But there will be occasions when they are the cause of problems: they can be associated with situations that were previously neutral but come to trigger alarm and fear responses. Thoughts and images, such as of a parent having an accident, can lead to anxiety. In OCD compulsive behaviours are used to allay or reduce the anxiety. The result is that as the anxiety is reduced the behaviour is reinforced and becomes even more resistant to change.

Repetitive and negative obsessions

Adela

Adela was accidentally pushed over in the playground and needed attention to a badly cut knee. For a short period she remained in school during break times. The day she returned to the playground coincided with a violent thunderstorm that frightened all the children. But for Adela it once again meant that she experienced fear in the playground. Staff began to notice that she was reluctant to leave the classroom at break times and seemed to look for any reason whatsoever not to go out.

Adela was beginning to develop a 'phobic reaction' to the playground. A phobia can be defined as the avoidance of a specific situation/event and thus the negative experience of anxiety. As long as she stayed away from the playground Adela did not have to face the situation that caused her anxiety, thereby reinforcing the avoiding behaviour.

Children with OCD usually have a degree of insight into the negative aspects of their thoughts and behaviours. This is referred to as ego-dystonic, meaning that the self regards these thoughts and behaviours as repugnant or inconsistent with the view the individual holds of himself or herself. This is why these children can be so secretive about what they do: they are embarrassed and ashamed because they know their behaviour is not 'normal'.

Because every child has a unique nervous system his or her emotional reactions to the fears he or she face will vary. Some children are more temperamentally disposed to anxiety than others. Being vulnerable, though, does not mean that the child will necessarily develop an anxiety-based psychological disorder.

Imran

Imran was 10 years old and preferred to walk to school with his sister than his friends. This was acceptable until his sister began to complain. Imran became upset and defiant if he was asked to go with anyone else. What seemed to be a childhood preference was beginning to turn into a problem. During playtimes he would seek out his sister to play with. He was becoming more and more isolated from his own peers.

His parents met with his class teacher and over a period of time Imran was helped to rely more on his friends for company. This was achieved through such techniques as providing Imran with a 'break time buddy' and teaching him relaxation skills alongside his peers.

You could argue that if Imran's parents and school staff had not been sensitive to his personality then he could well have developed an excessive reliance on his sister, which would have resulted in further difficulties as he moved towards secondary school transfer.

Obsessive compulsive disorders (OCD)

OCD is a condition characterised by recurring obsessive thoughts and/or compulsive actions. We all have some aspect of this disorder but, because we are able to keep the thoughts and behaviours in check, they do not interfere with our daily lives. Some of us have unpleasant or frightening thoughts that keep intruding. We are able to prevent them taking control over us, however – we are aware that they are irrational and should not be given the excessive time and attention that they seem to think they deserve. Others of us are more ritualistic/superstitious in our actions. We may be 'checkers' – we do not check once to see if the gas is turned off, or if the door is locked, but several times. Or we may play the 'symmetrics game' – if we touch one railing as we walk then we feel a compulsion to touch them all ('Step on a crack, break your mother's back', as the old rhyme went).

These patterns of behaviour and thought are common to us all; only a minority of people develop OCD to the point that it dominates and devastates their lives. Famous people, who sadly have the time and money to indulge the disorder, show how disastrous OCD can be if left unchecked. Howard Hughes is perhaps one of the most well-known OCD victims. His obsessive fear of germs, which began in his childhood, led to an adult obsession with cleanliness and ultimately to a sad and lonely life, despite his wealth and fame.

Most adults who suffer with OCD speak of it beginning in their childhood. It is something that they managed alone and often kept secret from their family and friends out of shame and embarrassment. Too often the reaction from others to people with OCD is 'pull yourself together', 'just stop doing it' or 'you really must try harder'. These statements are more of a moral judgement than an understanding of the difficulty – the OCD victim cannot just stop the behaviour any more than you or I can stop breathing. OCD is a disorder over which the individual is incapable of simply taking control without support and skills training.

In most schools there will be a few children who display the disorder. OCD has two aspects:

1   Obsessive thoughts
2   Compulsive behaviours.

Obsessive thoughts

These are usually ideas, pictures or impulses which are upsetting to the individual, who tries to repress them. Even though they are involuntary, the sufferer believes that he or she has no control over them. They are usually unpleasant, silly or embarrassing and they keep coming back, time after time.

Compulsive behaviours

These are actions that have to be done to a degree that is beyond their usefulness. Hand washing is sensible until taken to such an extreme that other activities are prevented. If the actions are not performed the child can feel worried, angry and frustrated. These 'magical' actions are undertaken as a way of avoiding some unpleasant consequence – the fear of dirt and germs can result in a pattern of compulsive hand washing.

While it is possible to have either the obsessive thoughts or the compulsive behaviours alone it is more common for them to coexist.

The following data were obtained from children and young people around the world who were diagnosed as having OCD. Thomsen (2001) found no gender differences.

Obsessive thoughts towards	Seen in % of the survey group
Dirt and contamination	40
Fear of something terrible happening	20
Illness	20
Death	20
Symmetry	15
Sex	10
Religion	10
Self-injury	8

These statistics show some of the commonest symptoms that children and young people with OCD display, but they fail to relay the depth and misery that OCD leads to. Thomsen (2001) describes the following two cases of OCD in children:

Jane phones home some 40 times a day because of her fear that something bad has happened to her mother. The phone call (a compulsive behaviour) gives her immediate short-term relief as she speaks to her mother. But the obsessive thought that something bad might have happened since she last rang leads to another phone call to allay her fears. Her thoughts and behaviour are dominated and controlled by the OCD.

John believes that he is responsible for accidents caused to people in the streets where he lives. To allay this anxiety he begins to collect all street rubbish and debris that might cause accidents. But after doing this he worries that he did not collect it *all* and returns to his compulsive behaviour which is constantly triggered by his illogical thought processes.

(from Thomsen, 2001)

While there have been reports of children as young as three years old showing OCD symptoms, these cases are extremely rare. The illness is typically seen in children between the ages of nine and thirteen. However, the younger the child is at the onset of OCD, the worse the prognosis for recovery (Skoog and Skoog, 1999, in Kendall, 2000). Therefore early intervention is strongly recommended.

2   What causes OCD?

There are many plausible explanations for OCD and the most influential of these are listed below. While research exists to support each one there is also contra-evidence.

Biological factors

Some researchers believe that OCD is caused by certain nerve impulses failing to control deep-seated behaviours. As a result, instinctive behavioural and thought patterns that relate to safety or grooming are released with no controls.

Yes and … neurological disorders and OCD are found to happen together when the same areas of the brain are damaged.

Yes but … why is it that children who have a normal development for a number of years suddenly develop obsessive symptoms? Also, children who suffer from OCD can have significant periods with no symptoms and then suffer a relapse.

Family influences

The families of OCD children can seem to be more rigid, with less flexibility in their parenting patterns than families with no history of OCD. There is often an authoritative style of parenting, with rules being non-negotiable.

Yes and … Adams (1973) found that there was a greater emphasis on cleanliness and perfection in the families of children with OCD.

Yes but ... Thomsen (2001) found that there were no significant differences between the parents of children with OCD and other parents whose children had a range of difficulties.

Heredity

Evidence exists to suggest that if parents suffer with OCD then there is an increased probability that their children will also.

Yes and ... if one parent has OCD then there is a chance of between two and eight per cent that the children will develop OCD.

Yes but ... twin studies have failed to provide conclusive evidence as to whether or not OCD is inherited.

Stress

Parents of children with OCD suggest that their children are prone to anxiety – a common feature of OCD sufferers – and that stressful conditions lead to the development of OCD. Some examples are family breakdown, changing schools, examinations and friendship disputes. Also, the amount of time that the OCD can take up can itself result in the child being under stress to complete all other activities.

Yes and ... a 1992 study (Rettew, 1992) found that 38% of patients or their family members believed a specific event preceded their OCD behaviour.

Yes but ... Chansky (2000) found that most children reported that they had 'low grade' OCD before a stress trigger led to the full-blown OCD. It seems likely that, while stress does not cause OCD in itself, it lowers a child's coping mechanisms.

In reality all behaviour is complex. It is best seen as being multi-modal – in other words several influences can be involved in producing a particular behaviour. An inherited disposition to OCD may need certain environmental features, including stress, to trigger off the behaviour. It might also be that there are a number of ways by which a child can develop OCD.

It is interesting to note that similar types of OCD are shared by people from different countries and cultures. Rituals around entering and leaving rooms are common; so, too, are issues about cleanliness and infections. Similarly, another 'popular' behaviour is collecting and hoarding. These activities are reflected in the behaviour of many animals:

- cleanliness, etc. – grooming
- hoarding and gathering – nesting
- entering and leaving – settling.

It could well be that, for yet to be fully understood reasons, certain innate behavioural patterns that are programmed into us all are triggered in some children for some reason and are beyond the child's conscious control. This type of explanation, known as 'neuro-ethological', is held by many child psychiatrists (Rapoport, 1990).

A further and more recent development is the idea that some forms of OCD seem to be associated with such childhood illnesses as strep throat and viral infections. It seems that, if children who are genetically susceptible to OCD have a strep infection, this leads to a part of the brain associated with OCD being damaged. OCD consequently develops quickly. Where OCD is triggered by a strep infection it is called PANDAS – Paediatric Autoimmune Neuropsychiatric Disorders Associated with Strep. Not all medical professionals are aware of this development.

Does it really matter if a child has OCD?

As with many disorders it is easier to prevent something early from developing into a more serious problem than to cure it later. It is clear that children who are distracted by their thoughts or habits have less free emotional and mental energy to tackle the learning challenges they are presented with.

Additionally, school staff have a genuine commitment to the 'whole child', not just the targets the child achieves – children are much more than learning machines. We are, of course, equally concerned with their successful involvement with peers and their developing a positive sense of self-worth. A happy child is a happy learner.

It matters also in the long run, as the following quote from an adult sufferer to a child psychiatrist illustrates:

> *Looking back, it seems that the hurt of an OCD attack was more psychologically painful than the death of my father, whom I loved. This may be very hard for a normal person such as yourself to comprehend. Nonetheless, it's sadly true. My sense of loss and grief was trivial and short-lived compared to any of the hundreds of OCD attacks I have had in my life.*
>
> (Rapoport, 1990)

The child's point of view

The real number of children suffering with OCD is difficult to ascertain because of their reluctance to seek help either from parents or other adults for fear of being judged as either abnormal or personally responsible. They often feel that they are freaks and that their thoughts and behaviour are signs of their madness. They feel ashamed and embarrassed to tell family or friends how dominated and controlled they are by the OCD. Children who are trapped by OCD are sad, bewildered and troubled.

> *My friends don't know that I have OCD. I keep it a secret because I'm afraid they will laugh at me.*
>
> (child with OCD)

Helping children to understand that OCD is not their fault is very important.

Key points for children and young people

1   OCD is an illness for which you are not responsible.
2   Think of the thoughts as if they were 'junk mail'. You are being asked to open messages that you didn't want.
3   Give the OCD a nickname: 'Mr Clean Me', 'Mr Perfect' or 'Checking Man'. You are not the OCD.
4   Practise what you would like to say to OCD – 'I am too busy to listen to you' – and say it.
5   Keep remembering what it is you would like to be doing instead of the compulsive behaviour – maybe meeting friends. OCD wants to keep you doing its work rather than relaxing with your favourite book or listening to music.
6   Show who is boss – do it when you're ready. For example, if you have to perform a ritual, do it when you are ready, make it wait. You are in charge. Try to not do it perfectly. If it has to be done a set number of times, do slightly less.
7   Keep reminding yourself of what you could be doing if you weren't indulging in the compulsive behaviour.
8   Keep a note of all those times when you do not have this problem. Look at what you were doing – where were you? Do those things that help you to avoid the compulsive behaviour more often.
9   Use the ten-minute rule. Resist performing the behaviour for ten minutes and, if after that time you still need to do it, then do it. Practise increasing the time that you resist doing it.
10 Get angry, get bossy with OCD; avoid feeling scared and trapped. The more you can change your feelings of helplessness, the better you will feel and the more able to take control of the OCD.

Parents

Parents can be unaware that a child is suffering with OCD. This can be due to a combination of the child's success in keeping it secret and the parents' not wishing to see it. The younger the child is, the more important and active the role of the family will be.

Parents will experience many emotions over OCD. Guilt, anger and fear are common. They know how to care for and support their child when they have a 'normal' illness – measles or a broken leg. But few know about OCD.

Key points for parents

1 OCD is a complex disorder and there is no simple explanation for why some children suffer from it and others do not.
2 OCD is nobody's fault. Focus on what you have done and will do successfully in bringing up your child.
3 Only share information about your child's OCD with those you trust.
4 Ask your child how he or she would like to be helped and supported.
5 Remember you are the executive – your child needs you to be in charge because he or she cannot control the OCD. Therefore taking a break and looking after yourself is essential if you are to give of your best. A stressed parent is not going to help things get better.
6 Keep focusing on your child's strengths and qualities. He or she is more than the OCD.
7 'Has' not 'is'. Your child *has* OCD – he or she is *not* 'an OCD child'.
8 Focus on your child's efforts and successes in increasing his or her control over the OCD, and give feedback.
9 Be flexible with your expectations, within a framework of consistency. Sometimes you will need to bend.
10 Take an active interest in other areas of your child's life, his or her hobbies, etc.

3 Assessment

How do I know if a child has OCD?

The most important question to ask when we are trying to decide whether or not a child is suffering from OCD is: 'Do the habits or thoughts get in the way of the child's academic or social life in school?' A thought or a habit indicates OCD if:

- the child cannot stop doing it
- it gets in the way of the child being like any other learner
- the child spends time and effort trying to stop it.

The four key elements of OCD

Use the following rating scale to decide whether a child may be suffering from OCD (from Rapoport, 1990) and score using Figure 1, p. 16:

1 *How much time do the habits or thoughts take up?*

0   none
1   less than an hour a day
2   severe: 1–3 hours per day
3   extreme constant intrusion

2 *How much interference do the habits or thoughts represent within the child's normal school life?*

0   none
1   mild
2   mild to moderate

3   moderate but manageable
4   extreme

3   *How much distress is being caused?*

0   none
1   mild, infrequent
2   moderate
3   severe anxiety observed
4   extreme, near constant distress

4   *How much effort is needed to resist the habits and thoughts?*

0   minimal resistance prevents the problem
1   some effort needed
2   a great deal of effort required
3   no matter how hard he or she tries, child usually fails

If the scores are 3 or 4 then there is a definite need to discuss concerns with the child's carers and consider referring to the school doctor

Common OCDs in children

Contamination
It is estimated that some 85% of children who suffer from OCD have some form of washing compulsion. Chansky (2000) provides a useful list of warning signs, some key ones of which are:

- long trips to the bathroom
- multiple and/or long showers
- excessive use of soap, towels, toilet paper
- avoidance of door handles, public toilets
- concerns about germs and illnesses
- avoidance of physical contact with others.

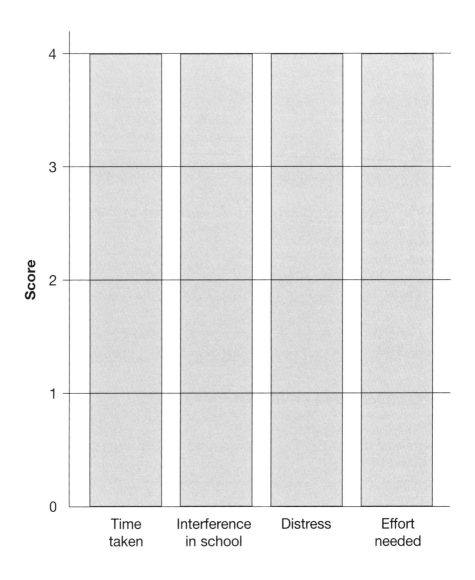

FIGURE 1. Scoring OCD: key elements

Iqbal
After a talk on Aids Iqbal began to become obsessed with a fear that he would contract the disease. Everything he did, the way he walked, the clothes he wore, the food he ate, all contained a threat to him of catching Aids. It destroyed his friendships and made his family life into a nightmare.

Checking compulsions

Ann
Ann was very competent at maths, but gradually her OCD led to her grades lowering. She seemed to need to check every answer two to five times on the calculator in case she had tapped in the wrong figures.

Rituals

Harry
Each night before bedtime Harry had a long set of rituals to go through. Each room had to be passed through in a certain way. His washing followed a strict set of guidelines and he had rules as to how many times he brushed each tooth. If he was interrupted the entire ritual had to be started from the beginning again.

Hoarding or collecting

Many children collect a range of objects, either believing that they will need them one day or that something bad will happen if they don't. Sometimes it just 'feels right' to pick things up. Steketee (1999) suggests that hoarding shows a cognitive blind spot. The child's thinking is dominated by the 'What if?' of needing the objects, which overruns the consequences of not throwing things away.

Hair pulling (trichotillomania)

Hair pulling is both similar to and different from OCD. They both demonstrate a compulsive aspect to certain behaviours and both respond to similar treatments. But whereas in OCD there is a reduction of tension through engaging in the behaviours, with hair pulling there is an enjoyable, appetitive dimension.

The possible causes of hair pulling are similar to those of OCD. Very young children may do it to reduce anxiety, while for adolescents it can be an over-learned grooming response. Whatever the cause, the difficulties and stress associated with it are self-evident. An adolescent may avoid many activities that would risk the exposure of their habit – swimming, roller coasters, dating, etc. The feeling of being different and the associated depression and lack of self-worth cannot be underestimated.

(The term 'trichotillomania' was first used in 1889 by a French doctor. *Trich* is the Greek word for 'hair' and *tillo* means 'to pull'. Mania is an abnormal love. Most hair pullers are female and this may be for social reasons. There may also be many male hair pullers, but it is much easier and more socially acceptable for a man to have little or no hair as compared with women.)

Whether the hair pulling is emotionally caused or whether it is mainly an over-learned habit, it does seem that the older the child is, the more he or she is able to develop more adaptive coping mechanisms. It is not uncommon for the cause of the original behaviour to have long disappeared and that it is now a response to increased stresses or boredom. Hair pullers frequently report being able to better control the habit the busier they are. But, like most complex behaviours, a range of interventions is usually required to overcome such over-ingrained behaviours. There are more self-help books available today, so that once the difficulty is out in the open there are proven ideas that can help a young person take charge and beat the habit (Keuthen *et al.*, 2001).

This is not an exclusive list of compulsive disorders. Children can create OCDs out of anything, from asking questions about the weather to coughing. Note how several will combine together – an obsession with cleanliness will often lead to a complex set of rituals.

A working model

Having explored common explanations for OCD it is important to draw some of these ideas together. This is more than a theoretical exercise. It can be extremely helpful for both the child and his or her carers to be able to make sense of what can be seen as bizarre or even insane behaviour.

Let us accept that there may well be a biological or inherited disposition to some children developing OCD. All children experience fears and anxieties as they grow and these can be coped with by developing certain behaviours that allow the negative emotional energy to be released. The behaviours distract the individual's system from the fears at hand, and the energy needed to carry out the behaviours dissipates the negative emotions.

Behaviours that serve such a function as allowing negative emotions to be avoided are self-rewarding. They are learned and, as they are performed more and more, they often become strongly ingrained patterns of behaviour – habits. This is OCD. The mind is scanning the world for potential threats and if any are perceived, whether real or imagined, then the anxiety-reducing behaviour is triggered off. Often the trigger can be boredom. When children are actively engaged in something they enjoy doing, the OCD is less evident.

Chansky (2000) uses the idea of 'junk mail' to illustrate the difficulties faced by the child with OCD. It is as if the child is forced to open junk mail – post that is rubbish and irrelevant. Healthy thoughts and behaviours do not cause distress; but the mind of the child with OCD has become over-tuned to catch and respond to unhealthy thoughts that can cause worry – I might get ill; my mum and dad might have an accident.

OBSESSION	DISTRESS	COMPULSION	RELIEF
fear of dirt	anxiety	hand washing	less anxiety

FIGURE 2. OCD profile

The obsession – the thought, fear of contamination or of being left or excluded – triggers off a *distress* anxiety response in the child (see Figure 2). Firstly because the thought has a self-contained fear element – being poisoned or left out, etc. is naturally scary. But there is another side as well, which is especially true as children become older: 'I am worrying about something for no good reason.' This in itself is worrying. Shakeela, for example, worried about walking off the pavement into oncoming traffic. But she also worried about having such irrational worries. To tell someone about her fears was impossible because she knew that other people did not share her fears.

The distress now triggers off the compulsive thought or behaviour, which is the attempt somehow to reduce the negative feelings: 'I have to wash my hands often to reduce the risk of being infected.'

Boredom as an OCD trigger

OCD can be triggered by boredom. When the child or young person is not fully engaged in an activity there is a danger that the mind might start thinking anxiety-provoking thoughts. As a way of coping the child distracts himself or herself by carrying out the ritualistic behaviours which serve to allay the anxiety. Some children will control the OCD to a certain extent by trying to keep themselves busy. While this is a positive step, it does not go far enough. Unless they actively learn to relax and cope with moderate levels of anxiety when they are aware that their thoughts are irrational they will always be prey to the OCD. They cannot remain busy 24 hours a day.

4 School-based interventions

Children and young people who suffer from mild OCD have similar levels of intelligence to any other group of children. They are as bright or as in need of support as the next. *But* when they are in class and being internally distracted by mental images and thoughts that threaten them with anxiety then it is not surprising that they are unlikely to achieve their potential. Similarly, if they are being pushed into carrying out a range of ritualistic behaviours, they will not have the same amount of time and mental energy for their schoolwork and friends.

(Note: children and young people with severe forms of OCD will often be on medication as one aspect of a multifaceted programme of support.)

In school the areas of difficulty are many and, as we have seen, are commonly related to:

- hoarding
- cleanliness
- contamination
- need for perfection.

Because of the amount of time children spend in school it is often there that a child's difficulties are first noticed. School staff need to be aware that a learner with OCD is extremely vulnerable to low self esteem; giving positive feedback on the child's strengths and qualities can help challenge this. There is also a danger of a child with OCD becoming socially isolated from peers, so classroom activities structured to include all are essential.

The effect of OCD on learning

OCD leads the learner to:

- have less free energy for thinking
- be distracted by the need to carry out ritualistic behaviour
- appear to be lazy and lack motivation
- have poor peer relationships.

Coping vs. challenging

As with most difficulties there are two sides to the support we can give. Coping means we accept the disorder and look for ways to minimise the negative effect of the symptoms, while challenging involves looking to remove the condition altogether.

Teaching the child coping skills

Here we can look at a number of appropriate strategies that minimise the effect of the OCD on the child or young person in school and help him or her to cope with the symptoms.

Perfectionism
A characteristic of all OCD symptoms is that they are time-consuming. Combined with the obsessional thought that unless work is completely perfect it should not be handed in, the stress on a child increases and, consequently, so does the power of the OCD. In order to reduce the stress the teacher should:

- set short assignments
- give clear time limits
- value mistakes as part of the learning process.

Cleanliness
Paradoxically, the freer children feel about being able to go to the toilet to wash their hands, the less strong is the need. When they are unsure if

they will be allowed they will sit and anguish over whether to ask or not. To minimise the anxiety in the child it is advisable to:

- negotiate a reasonable number of 'free trips'
- remove the need for the learner to ask for permission
- enable the learner to monitor his or her own behaviour.

Handwriting

This is an area fraught with OCD opportunities. Perfectionist attitudes can emerge, as well as rigidity over the shape of letters, etc. In order to reduce the potential stress the teacher could:

- provide a laptop computer
- allow photocopying of other learners' work
- set agreed targets as to how much is needed.

A useful approach to consider is *solution-focused brief therapy*. This is based on the belief that, because no problem is perfect (in other words no problem occurs all the time), when the problem is not presenting itself is when the solution is taking place. Whenever children are not involved with their OCD we should look to see what they are doing. Who are they with? Because people are too busy analysing the problem they don't notice these possible solutions.

Change is inevitable, but gradual, and if people are looking for the 'big fix' – the solution that removes the problem completely – then they will wait a long time. What usually happens is that problems diminish little by little.

School staff can help learners to analyse those times when they seem not to have the problem and when are they able to cope marginally better.

1. Who were they with?
2. What activity were they doing?
3. What strategies did they use to control the problem behaviour?

4. Homework assignment: *Between now and next week notice all those examples of things getting better*. This simple approach can help all involved to notice signs of improvements rather than only seeing the problem.

Cognitive behavioural therapy

The two dominant strands of OCD are the behaviours and the thoughts. It is not surprising, then, that the two methods of intervention come from:

• Behavioural modification
• Cognitive therapy.

These two methods have of late combined to become one of the most active and effective therapies to exist. Presented below are some of the key interventions from each. When a school is able to provide some level of teacher or support assistant time, then some of these interventions can be chosen and implemented with confidence.

Behavioural interventions
Exposure with Response Prevention (ERP)

This approach works to help the child break the OCD down into small parts that can be systematically challenged. The logic behind the behavioural approach is elegant and simple: 'if something is repeated enough times with no significant consequence, it tends to lose its attention value' (Toates, 1990).

Obsessive thoughts that generate anxiety are never confronted, because the compulsive, irrational behaviours reduce the irrational fear. There is no real link between the thought and the outcome; for example, the fear held by the excessive hand washer of 'becoming sick through touching things' is never tested because he or she is washing his or her hands all the time. If the learned link can be broken between the obsessive thoughts and the compulsive behaviour then the child will be gaining control.

The fear thermometer

It is important to grade the level of fear that children are experiencing; this allows them to see progress being made. The child can see the grade before, during, and after he or she takes control (after Chansky, 2000).

Step 1

Help the child to grade different situations according to the amount of fear they might cause.

10 Get me out of here
 9
 8
 7
 6
 5 This is hard but I can cope
 4
 3
 2
 1 No problem

Step 2

Work out with the child or young person the type of things that he or she would put at 10, 5 and 1:

10 ....

 5 ....

 1 ....

Step 3

Teach relaxation skills – breath control

Say 'relax' as you breathe in deeply to the count of 1–2–3 through the nose. Now breathe out to the count of 1–2–3 through your mouth. The breath must fill the belly, not just the diaphragm.

Self-talk

Practise positive thinking: 'I can cope with this,' 'I have done this before,' 'This is tough, but I can manage.'

Muscle relaxation

Work through the body's muscles. Tense them, hold and then relax, noticing the difference each time you let the tension out.

Step 4

The child chooses level of fear that he or she would like to work on. For example, if he or she has a need to count to 200 when hand washing, the child should work to break this habit, perhaps by counting in fives, or only counting to 150. Always start at levels that can be managed successfully. Child records fear level.

Step 5

Present child with the fear situation; child practises relaxation and records score.

Step 6

After agreed time – five or ten minutes – fear level recorded.

These procedures enable the child to see the fear levels gradually reducing as he or she is breaking the previously held associations.

Score

The level of fear the child felt before trying new tactics, how he or she felt while doing it, and his or her fear level afterwards.

Before   *During*   *After*

This approach is based on the proven fact that you cannot be both tense and relaxed at the same time. Therefore, by choosing a manageable level of fear, its control can be broken by pairing it with a new and opposite emotional response, namely relaxation.

Habit reversal

This has proved to be an effective intervention for a range of OCDs, especially tics. It involves the child learning to behave in ways that are opposite to what the OCD requires. It is explained in the following steps.

Awareness training

Children are helped to see the specific components of their problem behaviour and the usual places where it occurs. They perform and describe these behaviours. Sometimes observing themselves in a mirror can be helpful.

Competing response training

Children are taught a new behaviour, which is incompatible with the OCD. For example, if the OCD causes them to screw their eyes up then they would be taught to focus on an object they like and look for a fixed time without blinking. This skill would be practised daily and performed immediately after the tic occurred and just before one is likely to occur.

Motivation

This involves reviewing the inconvenience and the negative implications of the behavioural tic; these may include being stared at, being thought to be different, other children feeling nervous or frightened by the behaviour because they do not understand it.

Cognitive interventions

These involve children being able to express their inner thoughts. These will only apply if they are cognitively able to discuss their thoughts. Younger children will be less able to bring to conscious awareness some of the thoughts and beliefs that underpin their behaviours.

Thought stopping

'... stop ... think ... go ...'
Children learn to say 'stop' to themselves when they feel the tic coming on. They then think of something they want to do to distract themselves. They decide how they will do it and then go and do it.

Thought checking

Because everyone's thinking can be irrational at times it is helpful to teach young people ways of checking the validity of what is going on in their minds by asking themselves the following questions:

1   What evidence is there to support what I am thinking?
2   What evidence is there against it?
3   If one of my best friends or a teacher I like knew what I was thinking, what would he or she say?
4   What would I say to my best friend if she had this thought?

Automatic thoughts

Too often our behaviour and feelings are triggered by our internal thoughts, and these can often be negative, such as 'I will fail in this situation' or 'I will be laughed at by my friends.' Through practice we can learn to trigger off positive internal thoughts instead, such as 'This is new but I can learn to be successful' or 'I have learned other skills before, so I will learn this one as well.'

Positive thoughts

- How I see myself: I am someone who can learn new skills.
- What I like about myself: I am determined to succeed.
- Good things I will do in the future: I will take control of what I think and what I do.

And finally – a shared humanity

At the heart of this booklet is the belief that children and young people who experience mild OCD are only different by degree from others. We all share a common humanity. We all have some degree of OCD. Understanding the nature of OCD enables school staff to develop, in partnership with a young person's family, interventions that can prevent a mild challenge from becoming more severe and debilitating.

Further reading

References

Adams, P. (1973) quoted in P. Thomsen (2001) *From Thoughts to Obsessions*, p. 97. London: Jessica Kingsley Publishers.

Chansky, T. (2000) *Free Your Child from Obsessive Compulsive Disorder*. New York: Crown Publishers.

Kendall, P. (2000) *Childhood Disorders*. Hove: Psychology Press.

Keuthen, N., Stein, D. and Christenson, G. (2001) *Help for Hair Pullers*. Oakland: New Harbinger Publications, Inc.

Rapoport, J. (1990) *The Boy Who Couldn't Stop Washing*. Glasgow: HarperCollins Publishers.

Rettew, D. (1992) cited by Chansky, T. (2000) *Free Your Child from Obsessive Compulsive Disorder*. New York: Crown Publishers.

Steketee, G. (1990) *Overcoming Obsessive-Compulsive Disorder*. Oakland: New Harbinger Publications, Inc.

Thomsen, P. (2001) *From Thoughts to Obsessions*. London: Jessica Kingsley Publishers.

Recommended reading

Graham, P. (2002) *Cognitive Behaviour Therapy for Children and Families*. Cambridge: Cambridge University Press.

Martin, G. and Pear, J. (1999) *Behaviour Modification*. New Jersey: Prentice Hall.

Selekman, M. (1993) *Pathways to Change.* New York: The Guilford Press.

Stallard, P. (2002) *Think Good – Feel Good.* Chichester: John Wiley and Sons Ltd.

Toates, F. (1990) *Obsessive Compulsive Disorder.* Kent: Thorsons.

The complete set of titles in Rob Long's Building Success Through Better Behaviour series:

The Art of Positive Communication: A practitioner's guide to managing behaviour
1 84312 367 3

Better Behaviour
1 84312 363 0

Children's Thoughts and Feelings
1 84312 368 1

Loss and Separation
1 84312 364 9

Motivation
1 84312 365 7

Obsessive Compulsive Disorders
1 84312 366 5

Working with Groups
1 84312 371 1

Yeah Right! Adolescents in the classroom
1 84312 370 3